His

Love

Hurts

Vol 1

Jocelyn Ann Taylor

Acknowledgments

To my kids Joshua, Jordan, Jelani, Josiah and Joseph I want you to know that you mean the world to me. I gave my best to complete this first of many books and to be a better mom for you I love each and everyone of you. To the PURSE Foundation and Erika Lee I want to express my gratitude for you allowing me the platform to share my testimony. Thank you for loving on my family. To Michelle my sister I appreciate you for your support. To Eugene I appreciate you for seeing my potential early on. To Chad for encouraging me to continue when I felt like giving up. To Erica Thomas and Joyce Reed the day you ladies came into my life and showed me a day of pampering was phenomenal. To my friends and family no matter if you are near or far. The messages, the phone calls and support I received brings me to tears just thinking about it. Thank you

Table of Contents

Prologue

Reasons I Write

This journey of writing for me has been nothing short of a few different emotions ranging from excitement to sadness. At times, I felt I wouldn't accomplish my goal of completing this first novel. Being a single mother, trying to balance raising my kids in an uncomfortable low-income housing environment where it was common to hear gunshots ringing throughout the day and night; had me thinking maybe to follow the masses, conform to what is deemed socially acceptable. The gunshots alone has been a motivation to continue. To finish what I started. To help get my family to a better environment and find my independence through self-employment. I was coming from running errands one day and I overheard my neighbor speaking about making it out of the projects. You know get out of the neighborhood. She stated it is damn near impossible to get in here and make it out successfully. The systems provide just enough for you not to fall completely off. She also said she wanted to see one person who could build themselves up and get out of here on their own merit. I let that sink in. Could I be that one chosen individual to give hope to the other mothers? To tap into my gift and be a success? I used this as a source to not give up or settle into this unwarranted reality. I tightened my boots, prayed for protection over us and our place. I buckled down with my pen and paper or most times voice typed when my hand would hurt and now I can proudly say I will get out of here. I will make it better for my kids. Never lose hope and keep the faith.

Chapter 1

The Beginning

Ah man, this damn car gets on my nerves! I exclaimed slamming my car door. I walked around the front to closed the hood. It won't even crank up and it's too hot. I need my crushed ice. "Hey, I know a dude," Monty said. Monty is the neighbor from the next building. "He is reasonable and he does pretty good work on cars. I will call him for you." " Oh, for real?" thank you. "Can you see when he can come by because I got things to do. I really appreciate it." I told him. I hope this dude don't try to get over on me cause I don't have any extra money, I mumbled to myself while I walked backed to the apartment.

Monty came over to tell me his friend was on the way. I went to check myself out in the mirror just in case he was cute because I was single and ready to mingle. Hell, if he is maybe I could get him to go down on the price! I adjust my 42 DD's to make sure they were showing just enough cleavage. I applied my strawberry flavored lip gloss, and it was show time!

I walked out the door and the sun was beaming, barbecue-scented the air and he's walking to the parking lot. At first glance, I noticed the caramel skin glistening, nice toned broad shoulders, and a freshly shaved bald head. Not only that he was his own boss! He was making my kitty purr! Hold up... I stopped mid step because... well his eye was fucked up! Damn! I thought to myself. At least he looks good from the neck down. I remembered my first baby daddy told me to never trust a dude with a messed-up eye, but at this point, I gotta get my car fixed. I walked down the stairs and we greeted. "Hey, how you doing? I'm Willie." I'm hot literally, how you doing? I'm Jocelyn." I laughed. As we walked to the car, I walked a few steps behind him because I had to get that wedgie out. I'm not one to be uncomfortable. " So, what's wrong with it?" He asked. "It won't crank... like the battery is dead or something." I shared with him hoping he would be able to diagnose my whip. "Pop the hood and let me take a look for you." I unlocked the door and opened the hood. "Try cranking it now." He instructed. I did just that and nothing happened. Willie started working on my car then told me the alternator was bad. "So how much you think it'll cost, you know for the part, and can you fix it. "Probably about 50 or 60 bucks," he told me. Oh, I can handle that. I'm just glad you didn't say it was over a hundred. I said while I ran my fingers through my hair. "Let me call my homeboy so he can ride to the yard with us."

Willie, Brian and I were riding to the junkyard to get the alternator. My phone started ringing... ugh... it's this fool again. I ignored the call. He's calling again. I ignored it. Now he sent a text message. "Ugh, he won't leave me alone! Kendrick kept calling and it was irritating. I met Kendrick back in High School. He talks about remembering our first time all the time. He acts obsessed with me and it was only one time." A time I can barely remember really. "Aye," I said talking to Willie and Brian. "What does it take to get a dude to leave you alone?" They looked at each other confused about what I was asking. So, I explained that Kendrick and I went to high school together. "He found me on Facebook and he has been nagging ever since. I ignored another call. Willie said, " Hell tell him to leave you alone". "I'm trying, I've been nice, nasty, and nothing will work." Willie started to laugh. "Well, I don't know. That's a tough one. Do you have any brothers? Tell your old man to tell him to leave you alone". "My brothers only get in things if they're really serious otherwise, they don't get involved and I don't have a man, "I stated.

We were walking through the cars at the junkyard to find a used alternator and my feet were killing me... trying to be cute in my multi-colored sundress and goddess sandals. Those rocks were taking the life out of my feet, but I was twisting my ass like never before because I still needed the discounted rate for the alternator. I made it to row 16 and leaned on the first used car I could that was being held up with cylinder blocks and old tires. "So, Willie you know how long this will take to fix my car"? "Prolly like 20-30 minutes because the alternator sits on the side instead of at the top". "Alright then", while fanning myself with some paper. Row after row we check the used cars to see if they have an alternator. We finally found the part and started walking back towards the front of the lot. I was so relieved that this journey was nearly over. My feet were burning walking on that hard gravel. They laughed and looked at one another. "Y'all could have told me to wear tennis shoes" I frowned. We loaded back up in the car and headed towards home. The ride back was pretty silent although we were listening to some old tunes on the hottest radio station in the city V102.3.

"Okay, Brian now let's wrap this up, hand me the 8 by 16 so that I can tighten the bolt," Willie reached out while instructing Brian. "Hey, do y'all want something to drink, it is hot out here? We got some bottled water and I think my sister made some Kool-Aid." "I'll take some water please", Willie said. Brian just shook his head no, he didn't want anything. I walked up to Michelle's house to get some bottles of water and she asked me where they almost were done. I told her yes. Our children were running around me grabbing on my legs trying to get into the refrigerator. "Mommy can I have some candy or can you take us to Chuck E Cheese?" Joshua asked. "If I have some money left over Joshua we will see." I took the bottles of water back outside, Brian was packing the tools back up while Willie was looking around the engine.

"Do you see anything else wrong with it?" I asked while I handed him the bottle of water. "Everything looking pretty good, you shouldn't have any problems with it now". I was so happy! "Thank you!

I reached into my purse and gave him the money then we parted ways.

A young girl or woman should never have to flaunt herself to get anything in life. It's very important to have active parents/guardians both male and female or positive role models to be taught to embrace self-love also to ensure that she doesn't try to use herself as a barter. I know "they" say if you got it use it but that's not always necessarily true. It is best to pay for the services you need. You will appreciate it more. The mentality I had when initially meeting Willie was wrong but let's continue.

"Michelle guess what? I had a dream about Willie, you know the guy that worked on my car." " Oh Yeah I remember him." "Well, we were getting married. I was running to him in my dream. We were on the beach and he looked too good. Do you think he's the one?" "Girl, I don't know," Michelle said stirring the food. "Maybe you just had a crazy dream. What did you eat last night?" "Well. you know I can't eat chocolate anymore before I go to bed because I have nightmares. But I think I ate some peanut butter crackers. The dream was crazy; it was so vivid. I'm about to walk to the gas station do you need anything?" " You can just bring me some hot fries and some chocolate balls." "I got you I'll be right back."

Somebody got some music bumping today. I walked down the stairs and I saw the neighbors getting ready for the block party. It was an annual thing for the drug dealers to bring the hood together and give back in a sense. I didn't know it was today though I thought to myself. I rubbed my hair down because fly-a-ways were standing straight up. Someone was having car issues, and as I was walking I looked up and seen Willie and Brian working on the car. Brian saw me first and tapped Willie to get his attention. As soon as I was in close range Willie smiled and winked at me with his good eye. That caught me off-guard and I was blushing. I kept walking but why does it feel like I'm holding my breath. I rushed around the store to grab our stuff so I can bypass this duo and see if he would say anything. They had already left. It felt good to get some attention after having my daughter. I felt like a weight had been lifted. She had me feeling like I had another whole woman trapped inside of me! I'm happy with the breastfeeding though because the weight is just falling off and I'm liking my figure!

Ladybug (Jelani my daughter) had me feeling every hormonal change. carrying her during my pregnancy. It was like a double dose of a woman, If I was hot it was extremely hot. My crying spells were few and my level of sassiness was through the roof. I felt in my spirit before the ultrasound confirmation she was indeed a girl.

Chapter 2

The Hook Up

Weeks passed by and I hadn't seen much of Willie. "We have to hurry Jelani," I told my daughter as I pushed her umbrella stroller to the courthouse. It's a shame that I have to go through this with your daddy. He could at least help with something. Maybe clothes and shoes. I said to myself. "Gimme your baby doll I have to get it scanned." I placed it in the cart with my purse, cell phone, and Bluetooth. I gathered our belongings after the security administered a body check. "Excuse me, Officer, can you tell me where courtroom 2B is?" He gave me instructions while pointing in the direction we needed to go. I grabbed hold of Jelani's hand as we approached the escalator. In a swift motion, I scooped her up in my arms and ran to the courtroom. Whew. We made it before the sheriff close the door for the proceedings. Another sheriff instructed us to where we needed to sit before the judge came to the bench. I scanned the room looking for Dave and he was nowhere in sight. I snook and sent him a text message and he instantly responded saying he didn't receive the court order. I'm literally shaking my head. He was avoiding his response-bility as a father to her because I no longer wanted a relationship. Really, I couldn't call our encounter a relationship. Michelle was renting a condo and the landlord kept lying about if the place was under foreclosure. Later in court, we found out we had to move. We tried to find a new place but eventually, we had to split up. Tried to stay with "family" but that was not an option for me long term or temporarily. My job had ended and I resulted to sleeping in the car a few days then I opted to go to a shelter. We were among at least 20 other single mother families laying on a mate and a sheet on the floor. I was willing to tough it out until the rats ran through the place. I went back to sleeping in the car. I was hurt and cried a few times. I got this idea to ask for help on a site and some guys were nice others wanted sex for them to assist me. Jelani dad was one of them. I sacrificed myself. I was nervous as hell no lie to meeting strangers but I wanted a roof over my boys' head. I know you thinking "why you didn't ask they dads my oldest father allowed him to stay with his relative but that didn't last long. My second son Jordan his dad well let's just say he wasn't ready to be a parent. Jelani dad now claims he had a vasectomy. That she couldn't be his daughter.

"All rise, the honorable Judge Peggy Scott is presiding." She came in then we were all are seated. She announced a calendar call to make sure all parties were in attendance. "In the case of Patricia Williams and Mario Smith please come forward." This woman hasn't been informed of courtroom etiquette. She was sporting a baby phat matching short outfit with Jordan's popping gum. The dude was no better. He was wearing a white Tee and sagging jeans with some timberland boots on. "Ms. Williams, can you explain what the reason is for us being here today?" The judge asked. "Um, Judge, my baby daddy is court ordered to pay me $376.00 and he only gave me $25.00 two months ago, but he all on Facebook talmbout spending money and posting pictures with his boys in the club. Judge, your honor I just want Mario to do right by our baby." "Mr. Scott, what do you have to say for yourself?" eyeing the defendant. "Well, judge dis girl know I haven't had no money! Shoot my boys look out for me when we go out." he stammered "So Mr. Smith how are you caring for yourself? Where are you working? Judge Scott questioned him. "I ain't working right now. I lost my job with um the construction site." The judge looks over her paperwork. "Mr. Smith, it appears that you are in arrears and we need you to submit a payment today or your license will be revoked, you will be held in contempt for non-compliance of payment until the court receives a payment. What would you like to do?" His leg was shaking and he was rubbing his head before responding. "Can I make a phone call to call my momma?" The Judge studies him for a moment. "You may step out of this courtroom but don't leave this building until we receive a payment do you understand Mr. Smith?" He nodded. Then he stepped outside of the courtroom. Miss Williams, you can go and have a seat until the defendant comes back in the courtroom. she sashays to her seat while patting her weave. in the case of Daniel vs Hopkins please come to the podium. Ah man, this is going to be interesting. They were fussing while they were walking up to the Judge. she practically knocked him through the doors. Like they were in a race. Oh, my goodness, I can't believe this-this lady has a mini skirt 6-inch heels and her belly is playing peekaboo with her shirt. She tugged at it realizing that her muffin top was peeking out. It looked like he's been here before. He had a bit more sense when it came to his attire. He was clean shaved. Wearing a pinstripe suit with some Stacy Adams dress shoes. As they proceeded to the podium an argument started. "Quiet down quiet down Order in the Court," the judge said as she banged her gavel. "Miss Daniel please calm down and tell the court why you're here today." "Your honor, this man. This poor excuse of a man set up here and made my babies with me and then he don't want to help take care of them! I'm sick of his mess! All I asked him to do is to take Marco to get a haircut, buy him a couple outfits and he won't even do that! You know it's frustrating I have to sit up here and ask a man to take care of his kids. Your honor. Jasmine our oldest daughter is in extracurricular activities and I needed help paying for her stuff. He don't want to do nothing! He gets on my nerves." "Miss Daniel, please refrain from using the attitude while addressing the court. Things can go a lot smoother without it." The judge told her "Well, I'm just saying I didn't make those kids by myself and he could help." Oh, she better stop that sassiness before the judge locks her behind up. "Mr. Hopkins, what is going on between the two of you?" the judge inquired. He cleared his throat "Judge, whenever this girl asked me to help her with my kids I'll give her the money and she go spend it at the club, buying her weave and hanging out with her friends on my expense. I stop giving her money. I don't mind taking care of my kids but I can't deal with her and her childish ways. I don't even go pick up my kids from her house. My momma go get them because she always calling the law on me. I don't think they mines no way!" He scoffed. "My mama and my auntie said those kids don't look like me." "See there you go always including your mama!" "Again, yo momma didn't lay down with me! Ooh, you just wait," she interrupted with a neck and eye roll. I felt like I was sitting in the audience of a Maury episode. The judge banged the gavel again. "Order in the Court. Do you already have an open case with child enforcement Miss Daniel?" "Well… um what had happened was they told me to put in an abandonment warrant and then come back down there but I didn't have no way," She told the judge. I guess she doesn't realize that she's talking to a judge. It's crazy sometimes the things that people do. I thought to myself. "Okay, so I've listened to both sides of the story. Mr. Hopkins do you have any receipts to show for you caring for the kids?" she looked directly at Mr. Hopkins. "No, Judge I just been giving her cash." "He is lying! He ain't gave me nothing!" she interrupted. "See man I don't have time for this girl. She gets on my nerves," Mr. Hopkins said looking in the opposite direction. "You don't have any damn nerves!" Miss Daniel snapped back. "Order in the Court Miss Daniel please refrain from using profanity or I will hold you in contempt." "Finally, somebody gets her to shut up with her big mouth." "Mr. Hopkins, please do not blurt out," the judge instructed him. "Would you like to take a paternity test to establish that these are indeed your kids?" "I Sho will you honor. I don't have time for this drama with her or these games. My mom was right. I should have left you alone before Jasmine came along." Oh my gosh this was very entertaining. I hope she calls me up next cuz I don't want to be down here all day. I thought to myself. "Please go to the court clerk so we can get the paperwork squared away and get the paternity test schedule, Mr. Hopkins."

As I left out of court frustrated because Jelani dad didn't show up, I had to go through the process again. My phone ringed. It was Willie. "Hello," I blushed when I answered. "Hey, it's Willie, I was wondering if I could take you out sometime?" I'm shocked I didn't think he was interested. "Sure," I said, "I'm on my way home can I call you back when I get there?" He said it was cool and we ended the call.

I go to my kids' school to volunteer regularly. I didn't have anyone to come and support me during my high school days so that means a lot to me to be involved. Plus, it gives me a reason to dress up. Makes me feel like somebody special. The simple pleasures to enjoy. As I left the school I got a phone call. Oh, it's him. Let me check myself though I don't want to seem too happy even though I am that he's calling. "Hello", "Hey baby mama what are you doing?" "Hold on, listen." I started. "I want to be more than a baby mama so you can address me as Jocelyn right now." "But you will be my baby mama." he giggled. "Is that right? How do you figure?" I asked. "Because I can see the future" He and I started laughing. "Do you mean with the good or the bad eye?" "Oh, so you got jokes?" he said. "Well, I'm just saying since you talkin smack!" We laughed. "Well, I was wondering if you could come around here. I wanted to talk. get to know you a little better," he said. "I understand that you want to see me and I'm flattered but let me see if I can fit you in my schedule. You know I'm a busy woman. I'll give you a call back in a few minutes." I try not to let my voice get high a few octaves because he would know that I'm surprised or excited. I hang up from him smiling ear-to-ear. Let me call Michelle and see if she will look after Jelani a bit while longer. I'm doing a little dance while the phone is ringing.

I was looking in the mirror gotta make sure I have no eye boogers or crumbs around my mouth. I applied some lip gloss made sure my hair was straight because I know I'm finna get my man. It's funny though that I had this dream about this man and now he's here. I wonder how this is going to turn out. I know one thing though, He won't be getting no goodies on the first day. I knock on the door "Who is it?" I heard an elderly person. A man I think. I told him my name and that I was there to see Willie. He opened the door and looked me over. He was an older guy slightly hunched over. His eyes told a story. He had blue rings around the pupil and a nice dark caramel complexion as well. He was wearing some jeans rolled up at the foot and a button-down plaid shirt with some house slippers. "Hey, baby you here to see Willie?" "Yes, sir is he here?" I asked. "Sure, come on in you can go straight to the back. he's back there in the room." "Is it to the right or the left?" I asked. "Right there to the left baby." I walked on back and he was not in the room so I observed my surroundings. I saw a dresser, a full-size bed, a flat screen TV and the scent of black ice incense filled the air. At least he keeps his room clean. That's a plus cause I don't want no dirty nigga. I thought to myself. "Daddy who that is at the door?" Willie yelled. "It's the young lady you said was coming to see you." his dad replied. I took a seat on the bed and waited for him to come back in the room. I started watching the show In the Heat of the Night and he came in slightly wet. He had a towel wrapped around his waist. I looked and then I turned my head fast. "Um if you need me to come back I will," I said slightly startled that he came out of the bathroom like that. Willie laughed. "No, you fine," he replied. "I'm not going to bite you. I'm not trying to make you feel uncomfortable. If you want to wait in the living room until I get dressed then that's fine but you need to get used to seeing me like this because you will be my baby mama." "You know you always saying this whole baby mama thing what's up with that?" I stated. I mean... I think I'm worthy of being more than a baby mama and who's to say that I'm going to have your baby just to be clear?" I said. He started laughing again "Oh you will be." I got up and walked out to the living room. "So, are you Willie's dad?" "Oh yeah, baby how you doing?" he reached out his hand to shake my hand. "Yeah, I'm his daddy. Everybody calls me Mr. Frank.

You can have a seat." His father points me to an empty chair. "You look mighty nice today if I was a little bit younger I would have tried to talk to you myself he laughs I'm blushing I'm flattered. This guy is a firecracker I think to myself flirting at this age he is something else. We watched an episode of In the Heat of the Night and as it ended Willie walks out with brown loafers' light denim jeans and a plaid button-down shirt. He smelled of cocoa butter lotion and degree deodorant. I guess he's not big on cologne but I'm ok with that, for now, it's something about a good smelling man. "Hey, der Baby mama what you doing? "Nothing sitting around talking to Michelle." "You want to come around here for a minute," he asked. "Yeah, sure I'll be down there in a few." we hung up. "What y'all got going on?" Michelle question. "I don't know he asked me to come down there." "Well, be safe," Michelle said. "Girl you know I carry my equalizer" we both laughed. My equalizer is whatever weapon of my choice I use for protection. It could be a knife, it could be some mace. I grabbed my purse and walked out the door. As I got closer to his apartment I saw a group of guys standing around. Man, why he didn't tell me he had company already. I thought to myself. I don't like crowds, but it is what it is. He saw me at a distance, came over, grab me by the waist and he planted a kiss on my lips. That took the nervous edge off. I like a man that takes control sometimes. "Well, hello to you too," I blushed. Willie chuckled. "What's going on?" I questioned. "Oh, nothing much just hanging out with the fellas before we hit the motorcycle club for my potna party." "Um hmm. I see," I said while looking at the group.

Chapter 3

Moving to Fast

I was raised in the church, well in a few churches. I thought that the most important things were being part of a family, going to church, getting a good job and everything else would work itself out. That wasn't the truth. Life doesn't come with an instructional guide. One must go on their own personal journey to find one's purpose. It took this long to learn that.

"Hey, baby momma do you need to go and wash your clothes? Me and my daddy was about to ride to the plaza to go to the laundromat. "Yes, I do. Let me get everything together I'll see you in a few" I told him. I felt like the small gesture was nice on his part. He was being considerate because he knew I didn't have transportation my car was stolen. I gathered up our bags of laundry and he called me when it was time to come out. To my surprise, Mr. Frank was in the car I assumed that it was only us. That night Willie pulled out a pocket Bible while sitting next to Mr. Frank. Mr. Frank called out a scripture, Willie looked it up and read it aloud. At that time, I had never seen a father-son bond such as them in person. The best version I'd seen was the Cosby's. I felt that it was genuine. I thought about my parents and if we all would have been close if we stayed as a family. We dropped his dad back at the house first because we wanted to sit and talk in the car for a while. Willie told me that his mom passed when he was young and be was his father's only child. He made a promise with his mom and dad that they would always be together. I thought that was sweet. Little did I know the resentment Willie was harboring after being his father care taker since the age of fifteen.

Our courtship was a very short time. He was set on building a family and I was set on being a part of one. Jelani was only six months old when I found out I was pregnant. I was certain we would marry. It's amazing how your body goes through the changes and how you can feel another heartbeat beating inside of you. Pregnancy can be a beautiful thing. It can also be a little scary. I remember the first time I was pregnant I felt like I was an alien. I kept saying to myself that this wasn't right. It felt weird, but this time under the circumstances it was a bit different. Willie chose me as if he foreseen our future together. He told me I was pregnant. I sat there and thought to myself while I'm looking down at my belly, I hope this one is forever. This relationship. This Love. These were the thoughts that I had while riding the bus to an interview that I had downtown. As I rode up the escalator from the train, I saw a group of women a few feet ahead of me. I wonder if we're going to the same building. I pulled out a flyer that I found at the laundromat about a summer camp hiring and needing help. I was hoping to get a position as a driver. I saw a familiar face in the group from the neighborhood. It was Clarise. We both greeted each other as we entered the building. We stopped at the concierge desk to inquire where to go. After the interview, we went back to the apartments and saw another neighbor Shayna she was sitting outside with Clarise sister which reminded me of a humongous animal. I can't recall her name but amazon bitch was a great description. We were discussing how we were hopeful of getting a new job. I saw Willie ride by. I spoke out loud and said, "I wonder where he's going," all the women looked up to see who I was referring to. Clarise sister started laughing. The rest of us was looking confused wondering what was funny. "I know you not talking about Willie?" she said. I raised my eyebrows and confirmed I was. She laughed again and shook her head.

His phone was ringing and I was pissed the hell off. I didn't know what this chick problem was but I'm about to find out. "Hey Big Head," he answered. "No, don't you hey Big Head me! Are you supposed to be messing with somebody in the complex?" I asked him. "No. What do you mean what's going on? "This bitch got a major attitude with me and she claims that you sleeping with her next-door neighbor is that true," I asked him. "Man, you know good well I was not talking to anybody over here except you. I give folks ride sometimes and that's it. Who are you talking about though?" he asked me. "Man, I don't know this girl name! She got a sister that stay up here at the top. They say they from Jersey or New York. Some big amazon looking bitches!" I screamed on the phone. "Wait a minute now, baby mama calm down. I know who you talking about. She stays in the building across from me, but what she tripping for? She must be mad because I didn't give her any play. Just ignore her and go in the house with my baby." "Yeah," I said as I hung up the phone. I don't have time for this let me go take a nap. Shayna called me asking me can she use my baseball bat because some shit was going down. I got up, brushed my teeth, put on my shoes and grabbed my bat. Something didn't feel right but I walked over to her house anyway. I knocked on the door and Shayna answered and invited me in. Clairise spoke and her sister was sitting there with a mean mugged face. Shayna filled me in about some girl that she was supposed to been fighting about her baby daddy. I was not really paying attention because something didn't seem right. I looked around the room. I realized that the kids were not in the house so I interrupted her from talking and told her I was going to the store. That I'll be back. I opened up the door and walked out abruptly. I don't know what the hell is going on but they won't catch me slippin. I thought. I wondered did he sex this girl? I don't even know what she mad for but she ain't going to get me I say to myself. I picked up a few snacks and I looked in the bullet proof glass because they have some new items setup. I saw a knife. The handle was bedazzled with rhinestones and the blade looked sharp as hell. "Yeah, Jimmy let me get this one right here. I pointed to the knife that I wanted to purchase. "How much is it?" He flashed his flirtatious smile and told me that it was $12.99. I nodded to him that I want it. He filled the bag then he handed me my new toy. I held out my hand to get my change and stepped to the side to find out how to open and close it in case I have to cut this bitch. I'm satisfied with it and start walking around to Shayna place. I knocked on the door and Clairise came to open it. Shayna was whispering to the Amazon before she noticed me. I decided against stepping in and I spoke to Shayna." are you okay?" She looked around the room and spotted the bat. While walking to grab it she assured me the problem with whoever she was dealing with was resolved. She handed me my bat. I felt all eyes on me and I looked around to spot the amazon Clarise's sister eyeing me and then she sucks her teeth. "Aye shawty," I said "what's the fucking problem? You have an attitude with me like you fucking him or some. Is that it?" I'm asked her. Clairise speaks up before her sister had the chance. "Come on, Jocelyn I think you taking things the wrong way. You know what you and that guy got going on so just leave it alone. Don't even worry about any of that remember you pregnant," she said." No, but I'm saying like she keeps having an attitude with me! I haven't done anything to your sister." I tried to reason with her. "I'm trying to find out what the beef is but you walking around here like you don't know he been fucking everybody. You got yourself a trick!" the amazon yelled. I tried to push past Clairise but she braces herself with the door to block me. This big bitch has stood up now. "Yeah, I fucked him. I got that money too," She exclaimed. I was pissed off and I wanted to lay hands on her. Not for the comment but because I felt disrespected. "Hoe please don't get it twisted! He wouldn't fuck you with a BORROWED dick. Free me of the bullshit," I yelled back as Clairise closed the door. I started walking to Michelle's place while swinging the bat and her and my brother was on the balcony they asked: "what's going on?" As I explained, the amazon bitch emerged from the apartment. "There's that big bitch right there," I pointed her out to them. Michelle and my brother was in defense mode and was roasting her while she yelled back. One by one neighbors were coming out to see what is going on. I'd had enough of the argument. My words got tangled up with my tongue which frustrated me more so I start walking towards her. I was blocked by Michelle. She said she'd been to jail before and wouldn't mind dusting off the amazon bitch. Michelle was protective of me as I was of her. She told me previously if I don't have a record she didn't want me to get one over nonsense because she knew I would be successful one day. Willie was calling me on the phone. "Hey what's going on," "Man don't be asking me what's going on? You got here got me looking bad. Cause you fooling with this big ass chick!" "Baby mama calm down. You know you don't need to be stressed out while you carrying my baby." I didn't want to hear that. He called me back and told me to meet him in the parking lot. He brought me some cookies as a peace offering and swore he was not fooling around. "I don't want talk about that right now since we are expecting I think we should try something business wise. I took a business class in cosmetology school. I was thinking maybe we should open a mechanic shop you know since you know all about cars and stuff it would be good because you already have clientele. ""Let me think about it Joshilyn," he said. The crazy thing about social media is that it exposes you to a life that you assume everyone is having with the exception of you. You get all caught up in the glamor displayed Life. Your friends were either getting engaged or married, taking trips and getting promotions on their jobs and everything seemed to be going fine for them. You start wondering about your life what road are you traveling? At least I did. I was never comfortable but my quest for love took a toll on me. I was thinking that it would solve all the other issues in my life. For decades, our community has been broken partially due to the use of drugs and alcohol. Some adults do not take into consideration the effects that this will have on their children. In hopes of just having a good time. They were just living for that moment. When "that moment" end up being days that turn into weeks, months and even years causing them to miss tons milestones with their offspring. This was my case. Some parents realize and try to make amends with their kids. Some seemed like their mentality is still at the age of when they started abusing recreational drugs and alcohol. Speaking for me the experience of being in foster care and dealing with abandonment issues caused me to stay in situations that were unhealthy. The reality is you're just an adult with a hurt inner child inside. I know you are probably thinking "well that's your past. What does it have to do with you being an adult?" The experiences of my childhood influenced some of my adult decisions. For some reason, it is almost expected that once you reach the age of 18 and you are a foster child you know how to deal with life despite any hardships you faced as a child. Once I turned 18 I signed off the papers saying the state was no longer responsible for my care. I had to figure things out. This is in no way a blaming game.

I just want others to understand my story. The 14 years was not all horrible. I had a few good guardians along the way. So, I had to analyze why I was dealing with these relationships. In the words of my mom "you green as hell." To her, I was a bit naive when it came to dealing with life.

"You know what Joshilyn?" Willie said. Ugh, He sure had a way to mess up my name I thought. " I don't need this drama in my life. I don't even want to be with you no more it's over," with click. He hung up. I know he didn't hang up the phone in my face! Let me call his number back. Ring, ring, ring. "Hello, did you hang up the phone in my face," I exclaimed. "Yeah, I don't want to be with you no more. I'm about to go hook up with my new girl click. this is insane we were just together earlier today everything was cool so I'm trying to see you what just cause him to say this and hang up the phone in my face. I'm sick of this shit.

Okay, I got something for his ass since he wants to be smart! I don't know who he takes me for but he got the right one. Let me go over here to the store. I got a trick for him um hmm. I can't do anything too drastic cause I don't want to go to jail but Ima get him for fucking with me plus since beer seems to be one of his favorite things right along with them damn cars I got something. Just watch. "Hey, Jimmy let me get a pack of condoms. One with 12 in it. Don't matter what kind. Oh, and ring this up too." "What you finna have a party or something?" Jimmy asked. I giggled. "Oh, I'm going to have something," I said while smacking my teeth. I walked down to his apartment with my items in hand he going to learn to stop fucking with me. As I was walking up, I saw him sitting on the stoop in front of Brian's mom place. I politely walked past them and he chuckled. Yeah, I'm going to see if your ass going to be laughing when I get finished. Now which car I want to mess up? We got his dad's pickup truck, the blue Buick, we have the all black Chrysler 300 with the peanut butter interior it looks good but it ain't move nowhere and we have the baby blue Grand Mercury Marquis. I think that's what it's called. Yeah, I think that's the one I'm going to handle today. Willie and the guys were looking off and then they looked back at me to see what I was doing. I ripped the condom opened, popped open a beer and filled the condoms with beer. He got up and started walking towards me. Now that I have my condom balloons ready, I kind of giggled to myself because I know I have his attention. I started hurdling them at the Mercury. Here goes the first one. Splash! He was getting closer. The second one. Splash! I grabbed the third one and he grabbed my hand. I was able to throw it hahaha. Splash! "Man, what the hell you doing?" Willie said while holding my wrist in the air. I snatched away. "You called yourself trying to be a smart-ass saying you going to fuck around on me and you hung up the phone in my face!"

"I was just playing with you!" He said. "That ain't no way to play with me!" I snapped. You don't want me to come up to your sister house and mess up her stuff so why you coming down here doing this?" "Because you think it's okay for you to say anything to me and it's not!" I said with an attitude. "Now you see how I felt, Next time you'll choose your words a little better," I said and walked off.

Chapter 4

Just for Thrills

Me getting riled up had grown to be a thrill to him and his friends. I walked down the street I heard a horn blowing. "Shut the hell up!" I screamed as the car zoomed by. The nerve of folks there's not a sidewalk so I had to walk in the street. I swung the bat back and forth with every step. Somebody had the music blasted and it looked like a block party because everyone was outside. Empty beer cans and bottles decorated the street while smoke filled the air. He was all for a good time with the neighborhood. That bothered me sometimes why was he so connected to the hood I thought. People weren't reliable. One day they are here the next they were gone. I pushed through the crowd and his friend spotted me first. Cheezum was a like his Siamese twin some days. He talked a lot of shit and was the size of a twig. I cringed at the sight of them leaning towards each other to acknowledge my presence. Willie gave me a sly grin. Hey, Baby mama! Don't you fucking "hey me" We had plans and you with the bullshit! I snapped. I'm saying though why you come down here with the bat? It's for my protection why else? Well, Willie, you ready Cheezum asked Ready for what? I interrupted. Oh, we going to see some big booty strippas. No, the fuck you are not! I said eyeing them both. How dare you man I said directing my attention back to Willie. He seemed to have found my rage humorous. I don't see nothing funny you said that you wanted us to go out.

I wanted to believe somewhere inside he knew that I cared something about him and just words alone of him messing with somebody would easily tick me off. I guess it was entertaining for him though when I acted this way. I didn't really care though. Just don't think I'm some push over.

"Hey Willie, I need you to take me to the grocery store. I got to get a few things. "I'm not going to be able to take you. It's raining right now and my dad don't want me to leave him." "Okay, but yo daddy can come too. I just need to pick up some stuff. I told him. "Look it's raining and stuff out there. I'm not going to get out there." "Man, really? You act like you going to melt." I yelled through the phone. "Well, maybe I will but I'm not going nowhere right now." Times like this he really pissed me off. "You can play the neighborhood taxi, fix on folks' cars but when I say I need something there's an excuse!" I hung up the phone in his face. Lemme just go ahead and get on the bus cause I don't have time for this. I grabbed my umbrella and purse then I walked to the bus stop. It was only a slight drizzle. I listened to my music until the bus pulled up. By the time the bus got down to the plaza it was raining pretty heavy. I opened up my umbrella and looked down at my ankles. That baby weight was getting the best of me. I was swollen. I crossed the street and I saw what looks like Willie's Mercury. I was thinking to myself I know this can't be him. He just told me he wasn't leaving the house. First, I looked in the laundromat. He wasn't there. Then I looked in the pharmacy. Lo and behold he was walking down the aisle with some chick. She was a bit darker than my complexion. A whole lot bigger than me too though. They were laughing about something and as they were walking towards me I didn't know how I would react since I was pregnant but I knew I wanted him to see my face. I stood there until they came to the registers. Willie finally looked up and saw me. His mouth dropped open. He wiped his forehead and looked back down at the ground. I wanted to scream. Here I was thinking he was committed to me. I carry his child in my belly right at that moment and he was here with another woman. I turned and walked away from them. The tears were flowing down my face. I couldn't be mad at her. He was supposed to be in a relationship with me. You would think that he came after me but he didn't. I went on to the store to get the things that I wanted and came back out and they were gone.

I felt empty inside. Another person that I allowed in to knocked me up was leaving me to care for another child by myself. It was a gut wrenching feeling. It was never my intention to be a statistic. To be this mother depending on government assistance with multiple kids by multiple fathers. I wanted better for myself and for my kids. I wanted a traditional family. I guess I was so caught up in the thought of being in love that I hoped they would stick around like I do. Through the thick and thin. Through the cheating, through the lies but each time I was proven wrong.

My phone didn't ring for a week from him. I wondered if he would ever reach out to me but he didn't. I chose not to stay cooped up in the house any longer. I needed some fresh air and it seemed no matter where I was Willie and his new lady would pop up. I was thinking what the hell? How could you do this but I guess he really didn't care. I was leaving out of the hot wing restaurant and he pulled up with her. He laughed and said, "Hey baby mama." I didn't see anything humorous about the situation and continued to walk back to Michelle's place.

Michelle, my mom and Michelle's homegirl was there when I walked up. Michelle knew instantly something was wrong. "What's going on with you?" she question. "Willie over there with the girl," I said. "Oh, he is. Well, we finna go over there," Michelle snapped. "You don't have to do that. It ain't that serious," I told them. "Yes, it is because he thinks it's okay for him to cheat! You pregnant with his child. Come on y'all let's go there," she said. "Well Ima stay here cuz I don't have time for drama," I told them. They came back like 20 minutes later. "So, what happened," I asked. "Wait a minute," my mom said where you desperate or something I mean you got all this going on over here and he don't even look good," she said. I rolled my eyes and focus back on Michelle. "Girl, so we walked up in there and they were sitting at the little table. She looked like she was stuffed in there with her big ass but whatever so I walked up and I asked him what the fuck is up?" He told me "ain't nothing going on." I said "it gotta be. You sitting over here with this bitch and you got my sister pregnant! Yeah, you sent over here with a no-good nigga!" Michelle told the other lady. Girl, they started packing up their food and we followed them out to the car. My homegirl was sitting on his car when they came out. He gonna say "hey, can you please move," and she was like "Hell who gonna make me?" this was funny because she was a slim thick chick but stayed on go. She wasn't scared of nobody. Willie didn't say nothing and that big bitch that he with didn't say nothing either. Ma told him "my daughter had to be desperate to be messing around with you! You not even cute." this lady didn't have a filter at all. We all started laughing. "To me, he looked good from the neck down and it ain't always about looks," I said. "Well you know I got your back girl," Michelle said while patting me on the back. You know the saying love is blind? It holds truth. Things that I may not allow to happen to my family and friends I ended up tolerating it. I'm a big sister and whenever a guy has done some form of wrongness to my sister I checked him. There were no second chances. My mouth wrote checks that my ass possibly couldn't cash but I didn't care. They hurt her and I would make my mission to inflict the same pain. Now this situation was me needing a savior and My sister was all for defending me but I couldn't see this at the time. Remember I wanted this idea of a family I created in my head.

Chapter 5

Now What?

Knock, Knock, Knock. Who is it Michelle asked? It's Willie. She gives me a look of disgust because she had enough of the back and forth between us, she opened the door and told him he could stand in the breezeway but I've had the baby and he's slowly acting like he has some sense. I came to bring lil man some diapers and stuff he said while reaching for the baby. I grabbed the bags with my free hand and handed him the baby. What's going on with your sister why is she upset? He asked me. I don't know You know how Michelle is. I told him. Well, how are y'all is he ok? Yes, we, ok but It's time to start looking for a place because I can't keep staying on her with these kids and they are not getting along. We will figure out something soon baby mama he assured me.

Us figuring out something soon was not quick enough. The tension is thick for some reason and I try to keep the kids in the room because I'm not sure what's about to happen. Eventually, Michelle's kids make it known that we were invading their space. The first one burst open the bedroom door Gimme my toys that are not y'all stuff. I grind my teeth from being frustrated with the tick for tack behavior amongst. I rolled my eyes and instructed my son to give them the toys. He stood up reluctantly and walked towards my nephew to give up the toy. My nephew snatched it and ran out laughing.

Kids don't know how to express what's going on amongst others but they are aware. They sometimes can sense problems between people and will be the cause of heated situations because it's entertainment for them. I see why the elders removed children from grown folk's conversations. You'll see why too.

The twins come in the room next demanding to know what my kids are doing. I'm thinking to myself "why is she allowing this to happen? She knows the baby in here sleep. Well, I can't really say anything because we are living with them but it's messed up. I wouldn't allow this to happen if the shoe was on the other foot. I'm sick of this shit just picking and nagging. Look get out of here with all that I finally yelled. "This our room and our momma said we can come in here!" one twin said while rolling her neck and the other one placed her hand on her imaginary hip then licked out her tongue. I swear my blood is about to boil how angry I am. "Aye Michelle, can you please stop them from bursting in the room. This shit ridiculous. my baby in their sleep," I said with an attitude. She has to know that my frustration is not with her it was with the kids but the look on her face showed me that she was just as pissed as I am. "Technically Y'all in their room,"

She snarled at me with the raised eyebrow. I'm kind of shocked but not really since she had that chip on her shoulder when Willie came over here. "How are you going to say something like that to me I questioned her? I mean come on if that was your baby in there sleeping you would have a problem with it I snapped back, Really, I wouldn't be staying with anybody because I got my own place she said. The fuck does that supposed to mean I asked you act like I stay on you for free or something I give you rent money and I help with your kids. Well, Mama said you don't need to be here on me how she's going to dictate what goes on in your house? This was baffling to me. One of the only close relationships I have with my siblings, was Michelle and me. I felt my mother was trying to destroy it. Why was she encouraging Michelle to kick me out? We helped one another. Michelle interrupted my thoughts and said you got 30 days from the day to find somewhere to go. I cried after hearing it I feel like I was losing someone close to me but I sucked it up. I called Willie first. The only thing he said was so what are you going to do can't you help me try to get a place I don't know about that Joshilyn you know My dad is up at age he doesn't like a lot of noise and you know that's a lot of kids I paused and held the phone you waited until now to consider a lot of kids what you thought that they was not a part of me? I was furious! I hung up the phone then started calling around to the local shelters I scheduled an appointment. and they saw me a week later. As the day started winding down for my stay at Michelle's Place there was a much discussion between us until the final day I was packing up my clothes and stuff to put in storage and she finally came and spoke to me Jocelyn you know you really don't have to go I was upset because he done cheated on you so much and Mom said I interrupted her it's okay you know she was right maybe it was time for me to grow up and be in my own place this will be the first step and regaining My independence so I'm doing this for me and my kids my brother intervene he said man don't be worrying about What Mom said we family we supposed to stick together I know y'all but at some point I got to grow up. I'll see y'all later I grab the rest of our things and left out the door.

I wasn't sure what would be the outcome of us living in a homeless shelter but I knew I would give my best to provide for my kids. The staff told me the rules. There was a waiting list for the daycare so my kids wouldn't be in there right away. my oldest was in elementary school and they provided fare for us to get him back and forth to school until his special transportation was arranged. We had to be out of the building by 8 every morning and could not return until 3 in the afternoon. it was brutal for a while because It was the winter time and i had four kids to manage on public transportation. Since I had to take him to school we had to leave on the first bus which was 5:30 in the morning So that he can make it to school on time. Some days we sat at the library other days we sit at Michelle's place or Willie's if he felt like being bothered. Slowly things started coming together daycare was opening up so that I could actively look for a job to save up for a place for us I was so happy. I made sure to say my prayers and express gratitude for all the help that was given. Living in a homeless shelter was a humbling experience. All the workers are not kind. Some people even act like you were less than human because of the situation but most of all, there were other families there that could relate to our situation, Bonds were formed. Encouragement and support was given. Sometimes when I sat in there and felt so alone I wondered if God was even listening to me or hear my plea to help me and my kids. I stayed diligent in looking for employment. I signed up for the 6-week program to assist me with finding a job. It was helpful and I finally found a job. I saved up until I was able to have a deposit in a few months' rent and after seven months we finally found our new home. Willie Brian and my oldest brother helped us move into the house. I know After that ordeal; second chances should had been finished with Willie. I wanted things to work. Believe me the desire was strong.

Chapter 6

Starting Over

Reflecting back on a few things at least the last 7 months it was hard but I made it through. I was able to regain stability for my family, which was an awesome experience. We met a lot of new faces and I hope that we keep in touch. I was thinking to myself as I was doing the laundry in our new home. One, in particular, Torri was a young Morris Brown graduate. He relocated here from Tennessee to chase his dreams of working with inner city youth. He said that he would like to be a mentor for my boys. I thought that would be awesome for them to have a positive role model, as a matter of fact, I needed to reconnect with him since we were in our own home now to schedule an appointment. I reached for my cell and realized I had a missed call from Willie. I wasn't really feeling his shenanigans, he claimed we were not together and he stood me up because he was supposed to be taking me to work last week. Hmm, he left a voicemail. "Hey, baby mama I was trying to come by there. Maybe we could talk and I could cook some dinner for us. Call me back and let me know." Yeah, I'll let him know alright. He can wait on it now let me call Torri.

"Hey Torri, it's Jocelyn I was wondering if you could stop by for a home visit and we could go over a few things for the boys. I'll be off on Friday so I think that'll be a good time. Before noon if possible. Yes. that's fine thank you," I hung up the call and finish doing up the laundry before it was time for me to get the kids from school. I was so proud of myself. We were actually in the house. It felt like I was on my grown woman shit. I got my stuff together before I turn 30. It felt good. The neighborhood was nice, no drama happening, the kids had a nice size yard to play in. Now if I could just stay focus and keep things going we would be ok. I just hope that I don't have to depend on anybody because it's hard being a single parent and trying to maintain our stability with barely any support. Michelle would help as much as she could. I locked up the house and as I was walking to the car, Willie pulled up. What did he want now? I thought. He hopped out. "It looks like I came just in time. You didn't get my message earlier look?" "Honey, I was busy what's up?" I said. "I wanted to come over so we could talk. Maybe you can let me cook you some dinner. I want to make this right," he said. "Make what right? Do you. You said we were broken up." "Well, I'm saying maybe we can get back together. Come on baby mama. Don't do me like this. When will you be off again?" he asked. "Friday," I said as I started unlocking the car. "I have to go get the kids so your little pop up got to be short." I can't stand pop ups anyway. "Oh, you so cold," he said giggling. "Don't be like that I will make things better." we parted ways.

"Hey Ms. Jocelyn, how are you this morning?" Torri asked as we entered the house. We pulled up to the house at the same time after I dropped everyone off at school for the day. "I'm good Torri, how are you?" I asked. I unlocked the doors for us to enter the house. I placed my purse on the coffee table and proceeded to walk into the kitchen. "Would you like something to drink?" I asked. He said; "sure I'll have water." "Bottled or tapped?" "It doesn't matter," he told me. As I came back from the kitchen holding both of our bottled water. I realized that he was still standing. I guess I never really paid attention to him but he looked nice. Torri stood about 6'4, mocha skin complexion, low haircut, white crisp button-down shirt, blue tie, pressed black slacks with some shiny dressed shoes. He looked like a well-dressed NFL rookie who just got signed to play on his favorite team.

"You have a nice place," he said while looking around. "Thank you," I said blushing a bit. He pulled out some paperwork for us to go over for the boys. We wrapped up the conversation and I realized he was finished with the water so i reached for the bottle. Torri's hand met mine and we looked into each other's eyes for what seemed like an eternity. He loosened his tie. We stood up and he grabbed me close to him and went in for a kiss. My oh my this young man's lips were so soft. He thrust his tongue into my mouth and my mouth part ways to embrace this adventure. He was caressing my back and tilted my head to further seek pleasure in my mouth. Wait! Do I supposed to be doing this? I questioned myself. It was something different and new. I felt like I was a sleeping beauty that just received a kiss from Prince charming. I felt like this dude woke up something inside of me from that kiss. I slowly pushed back from him. I had to regain my composure. Did this really just happen? I grabbed our water bottles and walked briskly into the kitchen. As I placed the bottles in the recycling bend and turned around he was there. Standing in front of me. I was shocked. Really wondering how did he move so fast. Torri lifted up my head by my chin with his index finger and planted sweet kisses all over my face until he landed back on my lips. After what seemed like an eternity we finally let up for air. "I'm sorry I was so forward. I could not help myself, Miss Jocelyn, I've been wanting to do that for quite some time." "Well... uum... I didn't even know that you were attracted to me," I said "but it is refreshing. You do know that I'm older than you right?" "Yes, I know" he answered. "but I figure the attraction was mutual. The way that you looked me over," he blushed. "I didn't realize that you knew I was checking you out?" I said giggling. "Yeah well, I couldn't help but to see those beautiful eyes of yours." We stood in silence for a minute. I was biting the top of my lip. What was I supposed to do? I was thinking to myself. I mean he's younger than me. He is attractive though, and seemed smart but I got a ready-made family how would all this workout? A thousand thoughts raced through my mind. "Look," he said. "We don't have to do anything that you don't want to do but I find you very attractive." I said "ok," unsure what to say next. I came up with an idea but don't want to seem too forward, maybe we could watch a movie you know. I'm not used to having company. I just got in here. That can be entertaining while we get to know one another. "Maybe we could or maybe you can entertain me," he flirted. We shared another kiss and somehow found a way to my bedroom. He picked me up and placed me on the bed. He unfastened my pants and slid them down off my ankles. He then grabbed the seam of my panties with his mouth and work them down my legs. I really couldn't believe this was even happening, but I was here now. Might as well enjoy it, I said to myself. He planted kisses all up both of my legs alternating between the two. It was an amazing feeling. It felt like Heaven to me having his big strong hands rub on my thighs while his tongue pushed through my lips to find my clitoris and when they met I swear I heard fireworks inside of my head. Oh my gosh, I can't believe this was really happening. He swirled from left to right, then up and down flickering at a fast then slow motion while he massaged my thighs. His tongue then entered my womb and swirled around. Torri alternated from my yoni to my clitoris. The feeling became unbearable. I reached to put a pillow over my face to muffle my loud moans. Torri finally stood up to start undressing fully. I sat up to assist with the thought of returning the favor. He shook his head no. He just wanted to please me and I appreciated it every bit. He removed a magnum from his pocket and my initial thought was I hope he can fill it up. Quite a few guys carry these gold tokens and then they end up looking like a water balloon. He turned away from me and place the condom on, so I was not able to see the size. He turned back around and climbed up on the bed. He took my legs and spread them apart. Holding both legs up in the air by my ankles. Then Torri adjusted his hips so that his manhood found my wet warm vagina. As he rocked back and forth he eased it in little by little, with each thrust, I received a bit more and he filled my womb. I found a rhythm slow then he'd speed up. I didn't even want to scream this man's name but with each stroke, I moaned a little more. "Torri. Ooh... Yes! Oh God!" This is what it supposed to be. He scooped me up while the girth of his manhood was still placed inside of me and we switched positions. I was not good at riding and I think he could read the expression on my face. He took a moment to assist me with how I should be on top. I braced myself because I knew it was taking me places I've never been. He held onto my hips to guide me then once I caught a rhythm his hands explored my body. He closed his eyes to appreciate the moment we were sharing. It was satisfying, kind of like a breath of fresh air. Up and down our hips rotated together meeting each stroke passionately. He then pulled my head to his to share another kiss. I couldn't control myself. I started having multiple orgasms while his fingertips glided down my back. My juices flowed all over him and his face rewarded me with a smile of satisfaction. I laid on his chest and listened to his heartbeat. This was wild, daring, spontaneous and invigorating to say the least. We cleaned up and I walked him to the door in silence. "Hey uum, I don't usually do this but I really do like you," Torri said. "Well, I don't normally behave this way either but the feeling is mutual," "Is it okay if I call you sometime?" he asked, "Of course, you can after that performance I'm looking forward to some more!" I exclaimed We shared a kiss and I closed the door behind him. My thoughts were racing. I'm not sure what I should do. How I should feel. I felt excited, a little bit guilty because Willie was trying to fix things between us but look at how much shit that I had already been through with him. I save these thoughts for another time I need to take a nap.

Willie was calling my phone two and three times a day trying to make up with me but I was not sure this time of what was going on between us. I was not even sure about Torri. One thing I do know is Torri had made me feel special. That young tenderloin ignited a flame in me.

I got in the car to leave from work. I realized I had numerous amounts of voicemails and oh quite a few from Willie. only one from Torri. I listened to Torri's first. "Hey, Jocelyn I kind of have an emergency. I would like to meet up with you if possible. Give me a call back when you get this message." Without hesitation, I redial his number. He answered on the second ring. "Hello," "hey you, I got your message is everything ok?" I asked. "Yes and No. Unfortunately, I have to go back home to Tennessee. I have another Job opportunity with better pay and I'm taking it, but the thing is I have to leave in the morning," He told me. I felt like my heart sunk into my stomach... "I wanted to see you and the kids before I left if it's ok with you." Damn, do I renege on this guy to try to rekindle with Willie or play in the sheets with Torri one last time? I question myself in my mind. "Hey, Jocelyn are you there?" "Yes, I'm here I was just thinking how could I adjust my schedule," I stated. "I know it's last minute and if we can't there will be another opportunity in the future," He suggested. "No! I... I want to see you. Meet me at my place at 6." We hung up. It was so much I needed to do but I had time because it was only 2:30. I made arrangements for the kids to stay over to Michelle's because if this was anything like the last encounter I don't want any interruptions.

"Torri!" my kids shouted in unison. They were thrilled to see him, so was I. He spoke to each of them and asked about their day in school he gave a few pointers while we shared eye contact in between their conversations. It was 7:30 and Torri shared a farewell with them. I loaded the crew in the car to take the to my sister. I told him I'd be back shortly and to make himself comfortable. Now if I could get down there and back without seeing Willie I would be ok.

As I pulled into my driveway the phone was ringing. I was hesitated about even looking at the phone. Ugh! It's him. Willie. I let him leave a message.

"Baby mama I was trying to come through to cook for you call me back," That's one call I won't be returning. I had a prime rib in my house. I thought would fill me right up and I'm not talking about the food. I laughed to myself. I unlocked the burglar bar door he opened the main door. He grabbed me in and cupped my chin with one hand and kissed me. I liked that. This time my mouth was full of a fruity flavor. I slowly pulled back to lock the doors. "So, what was that, the flavor?" I asked Torri. "Skittles," he said smiling "Hmm... I just found out what my new favorite candy is," I chuckled while we walked to the kitchen. "Have you eaten?" I asked. "No, but I'm sure you can feed me," he teased while wrapping his hands around my waist. He moved my hair and kissed my neck. I spun around to embrace him and we share another kiss. We were interrupted by the ringer on the phone. He paused "Do you need to get that?" He asked. "They can leave a message," I told him. "Now, where were we?" I reached for his hand to lead him to my room. I turned on the radio to 104.2 slow jams. I took a few more steps and he picked me up carrying me the rest of the way. He laid me on the bed and kissed my forehead. Then sat next to me. "So, tell me why the sudden need to relocate?" I asked. "Well, things are not going as I planned here. I wanted to stay but this job is commission based and the opportunity I have at home offers higher pay and stability. I didn't want to go, but I have to do what's best you know," he said. "I understand. Lemme take a shower and get more comfortable," I said.

I came back from my shower oiled down with a black lace bra and boy shorts. You know that giddy feeling you use to get in high school when your crush finally notice you? That's how I felt. He walked over to me and planted a fierce kiss upon my lips. He sparked a fire inside of me. An awakening of passion that I yearned which somehow got lost dealing with Willie. He picked me up and I wrapped my legs around him while he walked us over to the bed. Torri laid me down and took a step back. His eyes danced with excitement. I felt a bit uncomfortable. It had been a few months since I saw a look such as this. I grabbed for the covers. "No sweetie," he'd finally spoke. "I appreciate your beauty. From the fullness of your breasts, to the stretch marks on your stomach, to the sweetness between your thighs down the curve of your calves. You are beautiful!" His way with words made me feel like a canvas at the art gallery. He climbed on the bed and licked my neck, swirled down to my breasts and popped one out of the bra. He took the whole areola inside of his mouth. Sucking on me as if to nurse his own stream of milk. With his other hand, he finessed my other breast out of the cup. He used his index finger and thumb to twist on my nipple then he alternated his mouth and hand between my breasts. The core of my being held a sensational heat. This dude turned me on. He stopped Only for a split second like he had an epiphany. Torri then licked down the side of my body, raised my leg in the air with one hand and used the other to pull my boy shorts off. I liked the dominant unspoken language. No schooling him was necessary. He alternated between licks and kisses up my legs. It was an unexpected arousal. A satisfaction I admired and appreciated.

After our sessions of lustful encounters, we quenched our thirst with fruit punch Kool-Aid and snuggled with each other while watching House of Payne. He raised up and asked if it was ok to smoke his cigar. I nodded in agreement even though inside I cringed because I disliked cigarette smoke and I hoped this didn't remind me of the horrendous smell. After that performance though, I couldn't be rude and have him sit outside. I think I heard a knock at the door anyway. I don't need that extra show from Willie. I know this would set him off. Torri would be leaving in the morning anyway and I probably wouldn't see him ever again so I was embracing the moment.

Chapter 7

Spaz Out

"Willie, I need you to watch the kids I can't cover daycare and maintain the house by myself," "Well I mean I'll do what I can but you know I have to look after my daddy," he said. I was irritated because he could watch them at my house with his dad there. "Look, I won't have them going back in the shelter. They had been through enough," I told him. "I know Joshlyn, I had grown to dislike the mispronunciation of my name. It amazed me how he irked my nerves now. "Jordan dad is in town. I guess I will ask him to look after them," I said. "So where will he keep them?" Willie questioned. "At my house!" I said with a raised brow.

"Well do what you feel, lemme get this food in there to my old man before he tries to beat me up."

"Alright, wait... Who's car is that just pulled up behind me?" I said while looking in the rearview mirror. "Oh, that's my girl lil momma," He said it with a smirk. "Really now. Humph, why you called me to give you a ride if you were expecting company?" I questioned. "She has to get used to being around you. You my baby mama so it doesn't matter. "Cool, I said I want to meet her," "Why?" "because you said she is your girl so I wanna see," I reached for the handle and stepped out. "No Jocelyn! Get back in the car and go home!" I started walking towards her car and he met me at the rear of the SUV and snatched me by my arm. "Boy let me go," I said laughing. "NO, I told you to go home!" He yelled. I continued trying to see who was in the unfamiliar car. He was behind me now and as I approached the car he placed his forearm around my neck instantly cutting me off. "Hold up," I thought. He was serious about me not seeing this lady. The car door opened and this lil momma hopped out. Short in height with a petite figure wearing a security guard uniform. Her face was puzzled by the commotion. "Get your Damn hands off me, Willie! What in the hell is wrong with you?" I was pissed. It was already a daily audience and they were standing at attention for the scene. Mr. Frank had made it outside shuffling around the cars trying to break up whatever this was becoming. "I told you to go home. She's my girl and we not together. You just need to accept it, Jocelyn." This dude deserved an Oscar nomination for the show he was putting on. I thought to myself. "You with the bullshit I see," as I mushed him in the face. He grabbed me with both hands and slammed me into the SUV. This was unreal. "I know you ain't put your hands on me I got something for you hold on," I reached into my pocket and grabbed my phone. "Since you won't leave I got something that will make you," Willie told me as he walked off. I was pressing the unlock code and Mr. Frank was trying to take my phone out of my hand. "Are you serious! Yo son just puts his hands on me!" For an elderly man, he had a good grip but I wouldn't let go. "Baby please just go home ok," he pleaded me. "Don't disrespect my house. I finally snatched away and got in the Expedition. I backed up into a parking spot. The hell is he doing all that for? I'm not with it. I said as I dialed 911. Willie came back outside with a shotgun. "Oh shit!" "911 what's your emergency?" The operator asked. I put the gear in drive as I saw him loading it. "Yes, I need an officer to the... Pow! I sped out of the parking lot. "Ma'am are you there?" The operator heard the shot. "Yes, my baby daddy just pulled out the shotgun on me. We had an altercation," I told her. "Where's the location, ma'am is anyone hurt?" I was shocked a bit in disbelief. I gave her the directions and waited in front of the rent office for the cops to arrive.

Days passed before he called me. Whenever he called though I answered. Things had been crazy between us but never to this extent. Why did he take it this far to be pulling a shotgun though that's what I wanted to know I answered "hello? "Um hey," he said sounded hesitant. "Don't call me as if nothing happened Willie! How in the heck did you think it was cool to do what you did?" I was choosy with my words because the kids were riding with me. "I just wanted to scare you," "For what though? That was totally un called for and you know it." Well I wanted to call and apologize at least. Time and time again I forgave him.

Chapter 8

Trying to Work it Out

"Hey, baby mama check this out I sold the Buick to the scrap yard." "How much did you get for it?" I asked. "Well they gave me 400 for it and I also got two guns too!" "Now why in the world would you want to go and get two guns?" We need it for protection. I got you a 22 and I got me a nine millimeter. It came with the bullets and everything!" "I don't think that was smart investment. "Well they got young cats moving into the hood now and I have to make sure that I protect my dad, you and the kids." "I've never shot a gun before." "Well I'm going to teach you," he said confidently. "can you let them stay up here at the house cuz I don't want my daddy to get ahold of them? You know he dealing with Alzheimer's," he asked. "Yeah that's fine make sure you put them in the back of the closet. I don't want my kids seeing it."

Oh, my Gawd, I can't believe I had a dream like this. Let me call Willie. "Hey baby mama what you doing up at this time of night?" "Man, I just had a bad dream!" "Why what happened?" he asked. "We were at a store and my back was up against the wall and you shot me in my chest but I didn't die. I kept asking you why did you shoot me. I said with my crocodile tears flowing. "Come on now you know I'm not going to hurt you. What did you have to eat last night? You know that chocolate does give you nightmares." he asked me. "I didn't have dinner. I guess I will go ahead and go back to sleep," "Everything is going to be okay," he assured me. "Alright well, I'll see you in the morning." We hung up the phone. Come to think of it I haven't had a crazy dream in a while. I know what it is. he's going to have to get those things out of my house! They must have got some bad spirits I thought to myself as I turned over and tried to go back to sleep.

"Willie, I think you need to get those guns out of the house. They have bad spirits." "Baby momma there's nothing wrong with the guns. You just had a bad dream." "No! I'm serious something is not right and you got to get them."

Trust no one

Trust no one trust will get you killed.

He said those words to me on a regular basis but I never thought he was implying to not trust him. You see during my darkest times of wanting to give up feeling like a failure amongst my siblings while still dealing with abandonment issues from my childhood occasionally, I would try to commit suicide. He was there for those times, there were a few times he caused my reactions to reach a breaking point. I thought to myself here I was dealing with another man had given him one child but I had a total of four. Those were the questions that constantly ran through my mind. I'd wonder why did this happen? Why nobody loved me? why didn't anyone stick around? I figured if I just settled and allowed him to do whatever he wanted to do that he wouldn't leave me sometimes he assured me that we were building a future together other times he embarrassed me, humiliated me in front of his friends but behind closed doors, He would apologize or act as if nothing happened then he suggested that I overreacted.

"Tell your brother to get the hell on cause I will shoot his ass!" Willie said as we watched my brother come out of the gas station. "Man, why are you tripping?" I told him as I wiped the tears from my cheeks. "He don't have nothing to do with this." Willie gripped the pistol a bit tighter looking at my brother then back at me. "Hey, Jocelyn what's going on?" He had a concerned look on his face. This was my younger brother but he stood the same height as Willie and actually favored me more than our parents. He was the hot head out of the seven of us. Always ready to pop off at anyone who crossed him. While his fight game is up from his childhood days I know he can't punch a bullet. "No, I'm good." "Are you sure?" My brother questioned me and then looked at Willie. "Yeah," I told him and we pulled off.

Trust no one Trust will get you killed

It's crazy he was constantly telling me " Trust no one trust will get you killed." I never thought it would be me he'd come after.

"Willie come and get me and drop the kids off to Michelle. I have to work tonight and I don't wanna drive in the morning." "What time do you have to be there tonight?" He asked, "Eleven to seven on this shift." "Okay give me a few minutes and I'll be around there," Willie said. Some days we be vibing things go good. I think he realizes we can do this thing called life together. Then it was times when he spazzes out on me for the smallest of things.

Chapter 9

Intuition

"Willie, I feel like something bad is about to happen," I told him as I felt an extreme sense of panic in the passenger seat. The thing is when I have had experienced these feelings before I would shut down. I would call off work and stay inside for the entire day. I had no one to discuss these feelings with my family because one; when it consumed me before I tried to commit suicide. Then two: one of the closest people to me suggested it was an act for attention. She said if I wanted to really kill myself I would go through with it. Mental health illness is one of the taboo conversations in the black community. We don't want to acknowledge something is wrong because we are told to pray about it and what goes on in this house stay in this house, but there is a hurt inside some of us from holding it in that it starts to come out in different forms.

The thought of being pushed back into a corner from life situations was overwhelming sometimes. I'd feel scared to live and be a part of the world but terrified to die. Something in me would say taking my life would make things better. Those times I could be calmed after a few minutes to a few hours through deep breathing and conversation. This particular time was different. I felt harm coming at me. It was like death was lurking around me and I knew it because my inner self-felt a sadness, a hurt that was different. Earlier that day in the back of my journal I wrote down my funeral desires with tear filled eyes and who I wanted my belongings to go to. I didn't have much but I was certain that I wanted my kids to have my valuables.

"Baby momma calm down nothing's gonna happen. Just breathe. You good. I promise," he said chewing on his tongue. "No Willie I'm serious. I feel like I'm about to die." Tears trickled down my face. "I think we should pray together." he side-eyed me. I grabbed his hand and we bow our heads. "Dear God, Jesus or whoever is listening, I come to you as humble as I know how and ask that you forgive us for our sins. That you watch over us and protect us and our kids. Thank you for providing food clothes and shelter Lord. Dear God, I pray in Jesus name amen." I wiped my tears away. Willie reached for my chin and turned my face to him. "You are okay you hear me. Stop worrying so much. You got this good job and I'm about to start working at FedEx with my cousin. Everything is going to be good. Remember you carrying my baby and you need to stay calm. He instructed. "Now go to work and I'll see you in the morning." We kissed and I hopped out to go to my post for the night.

I have to at least tell my kids what happened between me and their fathers I thought as I sat on the post. Maybe I should do an audio recording on my phone. That way they would always be able to hear my voice. Tears flowed down as I searched for the sound recording app. on my smartphone. Here goes:

Dear Joshua,

I was expecting to see you grow up and become a decent guy. I remember I didn't buy you a lot of toys to play with because I knew I wanted you to be a genius, well educated. I didn't buy race cars and play guns because I was told somewhere in my teen days that the material things come and go but knowledge was attained. It was in your brain and it couldn't be taken away from you. Leap frog was our best friend for your first years. Um, this is hard for me you know. Thinking of what I should say. I'm sorry that your dad and I didn't work out. To be honest, we had a pregnancy before you. I didn't give birth to her. Your father was not ready for another child at the time. He was very close to me. He grew to become my like best friend. We would get along most times. He was a gentleman to me. Due to the age difference, I believe that was partially the reason we separated. The other reason was the cheating. I received a phone call on your birthday saying you had a little sister. I think I was more hurt that I endured an abortion while another woman was telling me she had a child with your dad. I would wonder why I was not good enough for him. Either way throughout all of this I know he loves you and so do I. Make sure you help look after your little brothers and sister. Know that I'm always with you even if I'm not physically here.

Dear Jordan,

I was a bit skeptical about talking to your dad. We used to work in the same area. Occasionally I saw him on the bus and he used to just stare at me. I thought he was crazy. I'm laughing thinking back on that now. I spoke to Joshua Dad about dating someone new. he suggested that I give him a chance. Your dad started bringing breakfast and lunch to my job. He asked, if I made it home and how was my day. At the time, we stayed in two different counties. we decided to move in together, He's from South Georgia so he took pride in southern hospitality. He talked about marriage but as with all of us we have skeletons in our closet. He still had some that he wanted to deal with. We chose to part ways. Shortly after, I found out I was pregnant with you. I was Happy for Joshua to have another sibling to play with. I was sad because why I was only 2 months pregnant your dad got locked up and that was the end of the relationship. He got out when you turned two years old.

To my Jelani,

Unfortunately, your dad and I were never really in a relationship. I met him at a time where I was in the situation. I needed a roof over your brothers' heads. I met him online. We hooked up a few times. He told me that I could live with him. I chose not to, I didn't want to shack up with another man. Then when I found out I was pregnant with you I told him. He told me that he had a vasectomy so you couldn't be his daughter. For the first six months, he care for you then all of a sudden, he stopped. Your dad moved out of town. It was never my intention to give birth to you in a situation like this. My love for you is unconditional. Your smile brightens in the room and know that I tried my best to make him want to have a relationship with you. I even asked for DNA test he still wouldn't come around for this I'm sorry.

Josiah.

You're just a baby and probably wouldn't remember me but I love my chocolate M&M. I was currently in a relationship with your dad. we were engaged. He gave me his mother's ring. I was sure that we had finally got over all the bumps in the road and something great was coming about. I'm not sure what was going to happen, but just know that I always love you.

I suggested that we go on a date we made plans everything was set up for the weekend Friday comes along and he's flaking on me I'd never understand his reasoning to stand me up highly pissed, dressed and ready. I'd call this phone and Mr. Frank will pick up this had me furious Hey Mr. Frank is Willie around you? No baby you know he left out with Cheezum them. He said that they were going to the store. He's been gone about a good 10 to 15 minutes. When he comes back I'll make sure and tell him to call you." okay thank you, Mr. Frank, I hung up the phone. I don't understand men why you just can't communicate. A courtesy call or something. That bothered me the most.

I want to try something different baby mama he told me maybe we can try to work this out so we could probably start going on a few more dates what would you like to do? I've been asking you for a while I said to do something anything I like to go bowling and to the movies Maybe even go on a road trip I'm just tired of being Stanton Road. there's more to life that's sitting on the stoop hangin with the neighborhood and getting drunk I told him. okay well, I'll get paid on Friday will go up to Atlantic Station and catch a movie how about that he asked sounds good to me I told him. I was so ecstatic it's like he's getting it.

Friday is finally here and it seems to have taken forever. I going to get a new outfit from rainbow Got my nails done and my hair was already on point let me call him again and see what's going on ring, ring, ring the voicemail picked up I know good and damn well he's not sending me let me call back ring, ring, ring voice mail again okay well I'll just keep on calling Until he picks up ring, ring, ring "hello Willie what's going on?" I asked there's been a change of plans what do you mean well me and Cheezum them wanna hit up the Motorcycle Club it's my homies birthday so we gotta roll through to pay respect but you suggested that we go on a date so how you just going to switch up on me like this Look man. You got some friends and something you can hang out with he questioned me What does my friends have to do with you planning for us to go out? See this the shit I be talking about. I marched down to his house with a baseball bat I'm sick of this shit. He won't keep doing me like this.

I know you are wondering like why chase after this guy? Well I felt that he was obligated to be there. I'd giving him a child. Foolish of me I know now. I was sure this one would stay around. The other fathers got the hell on with no problem maybe just maybe he would finally stay involved in this.

I pulled in from work that morning. Willie and his dad was sitting on the sofa. "Good morning," I said and in unison and they replied back. I looked at Willie and something seemed right. "Are you okay?" I asked. "No, I don't really feel that good," he said. "Well after I drop the kids off at daycare it looks like you need to go to the hospital" "Now you know I don't do hospitals," "You are sitting up here sweating your eyes look yellow," then I felt his forehead. "And it feels like you running a fever. we going to get you checked out." After sitting in the waiting room for a couple of hours they finally called his name to go get seen by the doctor. I was ecstatic because I was tired. The nurse showed us our room and say that the doctor would be in to see him momentarily. We waited a few more minutes then we heard a knock on the door. "Come in," I said. Then walked in the female doctor. She verified his wristband and asked him what brought him in today. He said He didn't know what was going on.

He just didn't feel good. I intervened. I told her of his symptoms and she started looking over the chart. "It looks to me from the urine samples your liver enzymes are abnormal. Do you drink alcohol?" she questioned. "Yes, I have a beer every now and again," he said. "I think it'll be best if you leave that alone for a little while and you are running a fever? I'm not sure where that's coming from. She paused. "Do you have any other symptoms," He said no. "Hmm… well, I ordered for blood work and your test results won't come back for another 2 weeks. I will need for you to follow up with your primary care that's all I have for now," she said and walked out of the room. "Willie, I think it's time that you leave the beer alone. Maybe you had alcohol poisoning or something," I said. The ride home was quiet. it was getting close to the time to pick up the kids but I wanted to at least take a nap first. He got a phone call. He ended the call with "okay I can do that," I asked him who was it. He said it was Monty. He was going with him to work on a car. "Alright, you know I have to pick up the kids after school and the daycare by 6. I'm about to lay down and take a nap," I told him. "I'm coming in there too," he said with a sly grin. I was sleepy but I was always ready for our time together. Willie seemed a bit anxious. "What is going on with you? He was like a rabbit.

"Nothing I just want more of you that all," "Well you acting like this is the last time. Slow down it ain't going nowhere," I teased. We climaxed together. Willie rolled over then placed his hand on my belly." I can't wait to meet the new baby," he said. I was getting up to clean myself "Yeah I know," in agreeance. I started the shower and he came in shortly after. "Lemme get in with you," "You know it's not enough room for both of us in this shower stall," I told him he laughed. When we got out the shower we heard the car horn. He said, "that must be Monty let me get on outta here I'm gonna see you later big head," he gave me a kiss and left.

Chapter 10

Grim Reaper

It was almost time for me to go back to work Willie hasn't called. Lemme call him and see what's going on. I know he remembers my schedule least I hope he did. I called his phone it was just ringing. I hung up then I tried again. It was just ringing. No answer. I tried one more time and it went straight to voicemail. I didn't want to put energy into that...not tonight. So, I called and asked Michelle if she could look after the kids for me then I hung up. The next morning, I got the kids ready and dropped them off at school. I still didn't hear from Willie. I told Michelle after I drop the kids off we could go and pick up the graduation attire for the kid's ceremony. I told her that I wanted to stop by and check on Willie because I haven't heard from him since yesterday afternoon. When we pulled up his dad and his cousin was standing outside. I said, "hey what's going on?" They had a worried look on their faces. His cousin spoke first. "Man, I don't know what's going on with Willie. He's in there talking about its cameras in the ceiling and somebody was coming after him. He been picking up the gun and acting real throwed off. Mr. Frank started talking. "Baby I don't know what's going on with him. He just been acting crazy. See if you can calm him down please" I went in their house. I stood in the living room to call his name. "Willie." He came out of his bedroom. He was sweating. I asked him what was wrong He said he was set up Monty has some people come after him trying to shoot him so he had to protect himself. I dismissed what he was saying and told him my plans for that day and asked him to ride along. We stopped to fill up at the gas station and he pulled out the gun. "Man put that up!" I yelled. He said that he knew somebody was following him. With raised eyebrows, I was looking around trying to figure out what he was talking about. Michelle laughed a little and his father looked at worried. Next, we went to the mall. I told him that Michelle and I were going to do a little shopping. Willie said he needed to use my truck. I gave him the keys and got out. "I'll call you when we're ready," I told him. He said okay and pulled off.

A couple of hours had passed and we had finished up the shopping. "Michelle let me call Willie and tell him he can be on the way to come get us." We walked over to the food court to wait for him to pull up. He didn't answer. So, I kept calling the phone. Then he finally picked up. "Willie what are you doing? Me and Michelle ready so you can come and get us." "I'm not going to be able to do that," he said. "I'm just getting off the expressway. I was coming from Buckhead and a helicopter was chasing me." I was confused and hot. I didn't feel like playing games. "What were you doing up in Buckhead?" "Look it don't matter," raising his tone. "It does matter you in my car!" I told him. "Well, I'm not going to be able to come and pick you up." "You gotta be fucking kidding me. Bring me my damn truck," I said. " I'm not gonna be able to do that." Mt phone beeped then died. "Let's go ahead and get on the bus to go over to your house. Then I'll go down to his house cuz he's crazy. How you in my shit telling me you not going to be able to come and get me! He got life real fucked up," I told Michelle. After 45 minutes, we finally arrived at her house. I put down the bag and started walking now to Willie's apartment. I didn't knock the door was already opened. I asked Mr. Frank "where is Willie?" Mr. Frank said that he was back there in the shower. I bust open the door. "Where the hell are my keys?" Willie told me he didn't know where he put them at. "Just hold on a minute," "I'm not holding on for a damn thing!" I walked away from the bathroom and started looking around his room I picked up his pants. Grabbed my keys out and left out of the house.

My phone was ringing. I looked at the caller ID and seen that it was Willie. I answered "yeah." He said "hello," "yeah what's up?" I don't know who the hell you think you is," he stammered "But I got something for you," "he said. "You don't have nothing for me," I told him while rolling my neck. Then I pressed the end button. What in the hell was he talking about?

Chapter 11

Mad Man

"Have you ever seen the sky like this, Michelle? I mean, the sky is totally blue, it's so pretty, not a cloud in sight. A dandelion is swaying in the wind and catches my attention. She looks out the window and shakes her head yes, in agreement. "Before I drop you off, lemme check on Mr. Frank before Willie kills me," I laughed. "Girl, what was wrong with him yesterday"? Michelle asks. "Hell, if I know." I slowly turned into the apartment complex and for some reason, I feel like I'm having an anxiety attack coming on. The little voice in my head is screaming danger, but I ignore the thought. The notification on my phone warns me it's dying. Damn. I turn in front of his building and Willie is walking towards a crowd of people with a 9mm in hand. "What the fuck is going on"? Michelle yelled.

"Girl, I don't know but I have to get the hell on because I don't want to be in no mess". I pulled the gear in reverse. Willie looks in my direction and waves his hand for me to leave him. I continue to back up, then I looked at him and now he is waving for me to come towards him. I'm in panic mode; the Expedition is still in reverse. Suddenly my whip stops completely in the street and I looked forward. Willie is running towards us. He stops then raises the gun toward me. Pow! I ducked. I tried to crank the SUV again. And he runs to the passenger side of the vehicle. Michelle frantically tried to lock the door but she didn't hit the automated switch fast enough. He snatches the door open," didn't I tell you I was gonna get yo ass!" Willie said while raising the gun. "Oh, shit!" I said as I reached for the door latch and attempt to run but I fell flat on the pavement. As I stood up he'd made it around the rear of the vehicle on my side. I stand up and put both hands in the air to show him I pose no threat with this hot ass security uniform on. "Willie," I yelled "I'm yo baby momma… Why are you doing this?" I frantically asked, "Man you got to get the fuck on", he said. Pow! That was the loudest sound I heard. Seeing the fire come from the gun I put my left hand up to block the bullet. I fell face forward. There is a loud ringing in my left ear and everything is black. I looked up to see where he was and he is briskly walking then slightly skipping up the damn street. I can hear Michelle screaming "Why in da hell did you do this! Oh my gosh Jocelyn, it's blood everywhere!" I get up and get in the SUV. I tried to start it up again. After the second attempt, the engine starts. I'm in shock but I have to get away and the pain is… excruciating. I feel like my fucking hand is on fire. There is a hole through my hand and the blood is squirting out. I switched the gear to drive and we pulled off. I pressed the gas hard then I swerved around the building. Michelle is hysterical! "I can't believe he did this shit, Jocelyn look out!" I was trying to hold my hand up by the wrist and the police cruiser was headed straight towards us. I caught the wheel and turned it while I waived my bloody hand to get the officer's attention. "What happened, Ma'am?" The officer asked." I was shot" I yelled! "By who?" the officer asked. "My baby daddy! I exclaimed. The other officer asked where Willie was and Michelle tells her he went up the street around from where we were. She drove off. "Dispatch, this is Officer Smith badge 5632 we need an ambulance to the 1700 block of Stanton Road, we have a victim with a gunshot wound to the left side of my head and an entry wound through her left hand." Wait! Did he just say my head? I'm thinking to myself. I can still hear the ringing in my ear and a wave of sirens in the distance. One lady tried to bring me towels to apply pressure to the wounds. The officer stops her because they didn't know where the bullet was located.

The ambulance had arrived and the EMT asked if I can get out and walk. I shake my head yes while holding my hand to my chest. I reached up to wipe my head because I thought it was sweat, but it was the blood running down the side of my head. I climb on the stretcher and I face the crowd of onlookers who have their phones out recording the most devastating event of my life. These people... these social media vultures are treating me as if I am an exhibit on display at an art gallery. Tears flow. Not because of the physical pain but the humiliation; the embarrassment. These are people he considered his friends and not one attempted to stop him.

Chapter 12

What's Her Vitals

Beep... Beep...beep... beep...beep what's her vitals?
Dr. Paine asked. Nurse Banks reads the charts this is
Foxtrot 6179, Pulse 86, blood pressure 121/80, temp
98.7 and the patient is 10 weeks pregnant. Let's have
a look here she takes my hand and unwrap the
gauze. Next, she takes the dressing out of my head
to examine the wound. "what's your name love?"
Jocelyn Taylor, I stated. Well, Ms. Taylor, I must say
God must have kept you for a reason. I've seen quite
a few cases where the victim didn't make it. I'd say
two centimeters to the right and you wouldn't be
here as she pats my leg. Did we retrieve the bullet?
Yes, 9mm just above her ear Nurse Banks respond.
Physicians rush in looking astonished. Members of
the Crime Scene Squad come in to take photographs
while I lay in shock and excruciating pain. I've never

been one to like the spotlight and it has been thrown to me with no intention of releasing at this time. The ringing in my ear is still buzzing and the flash from the camera got my vision a little blurry. Ma comes rushing in. Where he at? did y'all get him? As she looks at me laying out over the stretcher. Cause I promise that mothafucka gonna get it if I see him. While we don't have the best relationship I'm kind of happy to see her. The doctor pulls her to the side to fill her in on the details. my thoughts are racing I'm not sure if a should be mad, sad or cry to express the gratitude for my life being spared.

Ma phone was ringing and she answered with an attitude. "Hello, yeah we down here at the hospital. Look Jocelyn is fine but she don't want y'all folks putting shit on Facebook cause this ain't everybody business"! Typical she got to have the spotlight meanwhile I don't know who is on the other end of that phone but I hope they know she's telling bald face lies. I ain't said shit because I'm not in control of my thoughts or emotions at this time. Dr. Payne comes back to give me an update on if surgery is needed. Well, love after looking at your X-rays shows that the bullet shattered the joint in your finger. You need a pin put in place but due to your pregnancy, I don't want to put you under the anesthesia. I think it's best to allow your hand wound to heal itself I know it's painful and we can't give you anything too strong because we want the baby to be healthy and as far as your head is concerned I will get someone from plastic reconstructive surgery to stitch that up ok? I nod in agreement with her. Dr. Kowalski introduces himself he's the plastic surgeon to stitch up the side of my head. Ok it looks like there is still enough skin here to mend this back together what I need to do first is numb the area around where the stitches will go this may hurt a bit but once the local anesthesia kicks in you shouldn't be able to feel a thing. Here's the first stick on the count of 3. 1...2... Ouch! I exclaim. The damn doctors never make it to the number three when they prick you. I think to myself. Every poke I flinched.

I was embarrassed for myself and my kids. I still had to be a mother taking them back and forth to school. People were looking at me crazy because of my wounds. Some would even ask what happened. I'll explain that I was shot by my ex and that he was under the influence I wasn't good at lying so I rather tell the truth. some people show compassion because they knew of someone or had a relative that had experience domestic violence others would tell me that I was crazy for even dealing with his family. Mr. Frank had nothing to do with the situation. He was an elder that got caught up in a situation caused by his child. He was heartbroken. So, I tried to help him maintain his apartment while trying to help myself and my kids keep our place. Eventually I lost our home and his father's conditioned got worse. He was placed in a home.

I don't really think that it registered that he had shot me or maybe I just didn't want to accept it. Two weeks after the shooting I asked his relative to have him to call me. I wanted to know why he decided that he would be my grim reaper and try to snatch my soul? I didn't understand how he could say he loved me but he tried to kill me? Who would watch after his father? Who would be there to talk to me? I felt I'd been disfigured. I had been through so much I couldn't possibly show that I was really afraid of him. What if they kept him in jail? What if they allowed him back out? The restraining order didn't hold up it was just a piece of paper. He would still flash the gun at me If he saw me in public. I had to keep a brave face when talking to him. I would ask what happened. Why was I shot and I never really got a definite answer. I don't know why I wanted an answer but I feel like it was something that I needed.

Tragedies to Triumphs

Have you ever heard the sound of a trigger from a
gun being pulled in front of your face? The barrel is
as black as new asphalt on the ground. The hairs on
the back of your neck stand straight up,
goosebumps form on your arms, and the loudest
sound in your inner ear is your heartbeat. I
remember that feeling. It's one I'll never forget. His
words forever imbedded in my mind. He said
"Trust no one. Trust will get you killed." The irony
of this is I let my guard down. He was the closest to
me, he loved me or so I thought, he encouraged me
and I trusted him. Then like the flip of a light switch,
I became his enemy.

I have struggled with sharing this portion of my life
because it's not comfortable. It doesn't feel good
being observed in a vulnerable way. I'm here now.
Opening up to share this journey with all of you.

Do you know what the word resilient means? The
definition is of a person or animal that is able to
recover or withstand difficult conditions. I like to
think of myself that way. I've overcome a lot of
obstacles and still recovering from this situation
which has been nothing short of being resilient.
Now I want to share with you what is deemed as

cliché, hurt people hurt people. That saying is true. This guy, my kids father was angry with his past and with time I thought I had enough love for him and myself. I didn't grow up wanting to be in a relationship or marriage being abused. My childhood was not pretty. I was dealing with abandonment issues because my parents were on drugs and foster care is where I spent 14 years. For some reason people think you grow up and there is no more hurt or pain from your past but there is a wounded child inside that needs to know. It's not their fault, it is ok to feel those emotions and it's also to get help and become the best version of yourself. My goal was to have a family something that I've always wanted. So, I decided that he would be my happily ever after. Now I know some may question "why did you stay?" for one I've learned a few things dating people can be an emotional rollercoaster because you never know who they truly are so you trust what is being shown or turn a blind eye because they offer you an apology and we are raised to forgive... Right? Dealing with this individual was initially sweet. It became worst when he felt threatened by me. Eventually, the ideal of me trying to achieve something better than what he was used to. After the honeymoon phase. He became a Dr. Jekyll and Mr. Hide. At first it was a mind game.

Since I came from a broken home and not having support from my family he used that for his advantage. Then gradually increase to verbal and physical abuse. I was in this situation and I question myself a lot. I worried about my children and their stability, then the finances. To have to start over weighed heavy on me. It is not always just a cut and dry walk away. One bullet from the hands of a man I thought I loved was tragic. Stripped me down from our home, loss of employment and the car was repossessed. Here I had nothing with my beautiful babies looking up to me. So, I prayed. Now I stand here with a second chance at life. Our own place, transportation and 2 businesses I'm building up, the chance to love myself, to love and embrace my family and to show you that yes it was tragic, but I am triumphant. I thought that this was love what we had with each other but the truth of the matter is love doesn't suppose to hurt but he showed me his love hurts.

Made in the USA
Columbia, SC
18 May 2023

16962510R00062